A Handshake From Heaven
Lesson Plan

Carol S Bannon

DEDICATION

This lesson plan booklet is dedicated to all Catholic catechists.

Through them, students begin their life-long

journey to knowing

Our Lord Jesus Christ through

The Eucharist.

CONTENTS

Author's Preface

" Train up a child in the way he should go; even when he is old he will not depart from it."
(Proverbs 22:6)

Preparing young children to receive Our Lord in the Eucharist is one of the most important tasks required of both catechists and parents. In this book are lessons I have used when sharing my book, A Handshake From Heaven, with students; adapt them as needed. If your activity adaptation is successful, please consider sharing with other catechists on my author page. We are in this together; to grow and strengthen our children as they begin their journey to know the best friend they will ever have … Our Lord Jesus Christ.

The artwork used with the activity sheets are provided for your classroom use only and are from the original watercolor art found in A Handshake From Heaven. These can be a standalone art activity or, when bound together, form a student's own Handshake From Heaven book.

God bless you as you spread the Good News to another generation of God's children.

Carol S Bannon
Author

"Upon the palms of My Hands I have written your name"
(Isaiah 49:16)

DAY ONE LESSON PLAN

GOALS:

To help children understand that authors choose to write stories/books about something they love.

To show children being Catholic is an active choice we make. It is a journey of discovering our best friend Jesus, and the Eucharist is the gift He gave us so we can know Him better.

MATERIALS NEEDED:

A Handshake From Heaven book
Multiple copies of Activity A:
Teacher sample of Activity A: *Prepare before lesson to familiarize yourself with directions*
Crayons and pencils

INTRODUCTION:

Have students sitting in front of you. When quieted, show them a copy of <u>A Handshake From Heaven</u>.

  a. Discuss what a writer does. Take responses.
  b. Begin a discussion about how a writer decides what they want to write about.
  c. Ask if they have written any stories. What were these stories about? Using the following conversation starters, point out how authors write about something they love.

Conversation Starters:

Ask students to raise their hands if they love to travel. Point out some people like to write books about different places to visit. (give examples) Ask students how many love their families. Point out some people like to write stories about their families and different things they do with their families. Ask how many of them love dogs and cats. Point out some people like to write stories about animals. Finally, ask how many of them love chicken liver sandwiches (or fried bologna, or liverwurst and olive sandwiches). Point out no one really writes books about chicken liver sandwiches because not many authors love chicken liver sandwiches.

  d. Point out the writer of **<u>A Handshake From Heaven</u>** wrote about something she loves. She wrote this book because she loves being Catholic.

LESSON: Tell the students: *I am Catholic too, just like the author, and I want to tell you why I love being Catholic.*

Being Catholic means you are on a *journey* of getting to know your best friend. (**Ask: "who is this best friend we all want to know?"- *Jesus*)**- and every journey we take begins with a first step.

1. Baptism is every Catholic's first step – Explain how your parents brought you to their Catholic Church and baptized you. You became part of the Church…you were baptized Catholic!
2. Other people, like your grandparents, teachers, coaches, aunts and uncles, all taught you something more about your best friend Jesus.
3. Explain how in Second Grade you made your First Reconciliation, just like they will. Remind them that Jesus, their best friend, loves them "**no matter what**"…He will always forgive, **no matter what.**

Additional Discussion Ideas

Give a few funny examples of things you did at their age that you were later sorry about; for example, you broke your mother's favorite vase and blamed it on your younger brother because he couldn't talk yet. You were sorry because you saw how upset your mother was. Jesus forgave you even though it may have taken your mother longer to say it was okay! Or maybe you hid your sister's glasses and laughed while she got all upset and started running around the house looking for them – they were sitting at the bottom of her book bag where you had hidden them. Even though your sister didn't forgive you, Jesus did. Tell them we all do things we are not proud of, and yet our best friend Jesus forgives us when we are sorry and continues to love us **no matter what**!

<u>LESSON ACTIVITY</u>: Role Playing

Tell students to picture themselves on a playground and a group of bullies are saying really mean things about a specific person. You walk up to the swings, trying to avoid them because they are picking on a friend of yours. They stop you from going to the swings, surround you,. point their fingers and say (walk up to a student in your circle and point your finger at him/her)" *Hey-you know this person don't you?"*See how this child reacts. Then go to another student in your circle and say "*Hey, I've seen you playing with this person…you do play with him don't you?"*Do this a few times and discuss the different reactions to being accused of playing with someone who is not well liked.

Explain how easy it is to just say *"No, I don't know him. I don't ever play with him."*

Ask them to imagine how St. Peter must have felt on Holy Thursday night when the people came up and accused him of knowing Jesus. Ask them what St. Peter did when he was accused of knowing Jesus. *(Take all responses, but remind them that St. Peter acted as many of us would do – he denied knowing Jesus)* Then tell your students that Jesus not only forgave St. Peter, He told St. Peter "You are Peter and upon this rock I will build my Church". (Matthew 16:18)

Explain how Jesus and Peter were best friends. Explain Jesus IS the best friend any of us will ever have because He forgives us ANYTHING.

Teach them the Sacrament of the Eucharist is our gift from Jesus. It is a gift from our best friend and the next step in our journey to get to know our best friend JESUS.

ART ACTIVITY: Hand out copies of Activity A. (*An alternative activity may be to hand out blank pieces of papers and have the students trace their own hand and complete the sentence on their own*) Explain they are to fill in the handprint with some of the things Jesus already knows about them.

   a. Using your sample handprint, explain that every fact you wrote down about yourself is one Jesus already knows about you.
   b. Next, brainstorm some of the things Jesus already knows about them. These can include their favorite sport, their hair color, the names of their brothers and sisters, their pets, where they live, their favorite food, the color of their house: be creative.
   c. Allow the students to fill in their art activity and color the surrounding area.
   d. Complete the sentence: I want to reach out for Jesus because _____.

CONCLUSION: Collect the art activity. Ask for a few volunteers to share their completed sentence. Explain that Jesus knows each and every one of us already. It is now our job to get to know Jesus, and we can do this by receiving Him in the Sacrament of the Holy Eucharist.

Notes:

"So, whether you eat or drink, or whatever you do, do all to the glory of God"

(Corinthians 10:31)

DAY TWO LESSON PLAN

GOAL: To show children the best way to get to know their friend Jesus is by spending time every week with Him.

MATERIALS:

A Handshake From Heaven book
Plastic zip lock bag filled with 168 pieces of small candy or other small items
Student art activity from Day One
Copies of Activity B
Crayons and pencils

INTRODUCTION: Walk around your group and shake their hands. Introduce yourself again. Tell them to shake one another's hands. Go back to one of the students and shake their hand again.

   a. Discuss why adults shake hands with other people.
   b. Possible answers could include:
      1. to introduce themselves to a stranger
      2. to make someone feel welcome
      3. to invite a person into their house
      4.   to say "Hi!" to a friend.
      5. to give the sign of peace in Church.

LESSON: Recall Lesson One's Art Activity by reading out loud a few of the palm descriptions that the students filled out. Have the class try to guess whose palm you are reading. After doing a few of these explain that God gave each one of them special gifts. He knows what these gifts are because He is the One who gave them.

   a. Ask: "**What do adults do when they want to get to know someone?**
   b. Lead them to understand most adults begin with shaking hands; they hold hands with other people
   c. Tell them "**God already knows us. He wants us to get to know Him.**"
   d. Explain: "When you receive the Eucharist you will be holding Jesus' Body in your hands."

LESSON ACTIVITY: (*The following has been used multiple times across the country to emphasize the need for taking time each week to attend Mass. Feel free to use verbatim or modify as you see fit.*)

   a. Explain you are going to tell them a story about a teacher named Sister Mary Margaret Catherine.
      1. Sister Mary Margaret Catherine told her class one day to close their eyes because she had something very important to share with them. (Tell your class to close their eyes, put their heads down and just listen)
      2. This is what Sister Mary Margaret Catherine told her class to do: "*Imagine a beautiful day filled with all the things children love to do – the same things many of you said you loved to do when we talked about writing stories. Imagine playing soccer, or basketball, cheerleading, dancing, running, laughing, cooking, playing games*

with your families, doing homework (well, maybe not homework) – all the things we love to do during one single day".

   3. Be silent for a few seconds before continuing: *"Then Sr. Mary Margaret Catherine told us to keep our eyes closed while she put something on each one of our desks."*

b. Bring out the bag filled with 168 pieces of candy and tell the students to open their eyes. *"This is what Sr. Mary Margaret Catherine put on each one of her student's desks. She put a bag filled with 168 pieces of candy on everyone's desk. Wasn't she the best teacher ever?"*

c. Explain how heavy a bag of 168 pieces of candy can be. Have a student come up and hold the bag of candy. Keep reinforcing the number 168.

d. Now ask **"How many days are there in one week?"**

e. Then ask: **"Can anyone guess how many hours there are in one week?"** (168)

f. Explain how Jesus gives us 168 hours every week to do whatever we want to do, whatever we love to do – (give examples again of all the things children fill their days doing)

g. All He asks from us is one hour (take one piece of candy out of the bag and set it near the filled bag). All the other 167 pieces/hours are ours; we can do whatever we want to do, love to do, or need to do. **ACTION**: Take the one piece of candy in one hand, the filled bag of candy in the other to demonstrate that all God wants from us is one single hour a week. He wants us to come to Mass. He gave us the Mass so we can get to know Jesus.

<u>ART ACTIVITY</u>: Hand out copies of Activity B.

a. Discuss how it does not matter how old we are, how we are dressed, or what we look like. All God wants is for us to come to His Church and get to know Jesus.

b. Have students complete the sentence: I will come to your table Jesus because____.

c. Color and collect when completed.

Notes:

"This is my body, which is given for you. Do this in remembrance of me."

(Luke 22:19)

DAY THREE LESSON PLAN

GOAL: To integrate the idea behind God's feast and why coming to His table is central in our journey as Catholics to knowing Jesus.

MATERIALS:

A Handshake From Heaven book
Bag of candy from Day Two Lesson Plan
Activity C copies.
Pencils and Crayons/Markers

INTRODUCTION: Bring out the bag of 168 pieces of candy. Ask if anyone remembers why Sister Mary Margaret Catherine put a bag on each one of her student's desks. Remind your class how Jesus invites us to His Table. He wants us to come to His table and share in the meal that He has prepared for us.

LESSON: Brainstorm all the steps of getting ready for a huge celebration such as Christmas, birthday parties, or a party to celebrate their First Holy Communion.

   a. Some ideas may include:
       1. Cleaning the house
       2. Shopping for the food
       3. Cooking all the food
       4. Ordering a cake
       5. Inviting the people to come
       6. Maybe shopping for new clothes
       7. Putting all the food out for the guests
       8. Getting all dressed up for the party to begin
   b. Now instruct the class to close their eyes and imagine how they will feel waiting for their guests to arrive so the party can begin. And waiting and waiting for the doorbell to ring, but no one is ringing the doorbell.
   c. Ask them to open their eyes and tell you how they would feel if no one bothered to come to the party they just spent all this time preparing for.
   d. Explain: **"Every week Jesus invites us to His table…every week Jesus gives us the opportunity to get to know Him just a little bit better. I made my First Communion a long long long – really long time ago- boys and girls – and yet every time I go up to His table I get to know Him a little bit better."**

ADDITIONAL LESSON ACTIVITY: *Role Playing being the new student at a school.*

Ask if anyone has ever had to go to a new school and been told to sit at a specific table filled with strangers for lunch.

a. Choose five students. One will be the new student at school, and the other four will be good friends at the school lunch table

b. Have the four students at the table talking and laughing. Walk up to the "new student" and order him/her to sit at "that" table – pointing to the table of four friends.

c. Ask how the "new" student feels walking up this table filled with strangers.

d. Repeat the exercise a few times until the "new" student isn't "new" any longer.

e. When the students come back to the circle explain how after meeting people every day, sitting down at the same table with them every day, you get to know them. You are no longer shy or afraid because you are making friend.

f. Explain to the class this is why we walk up to the Lord's Table as often as we can. We want to get to know our best friend Jesus. Remind the students the writer of A Handshake From Heaven wrote the book to show that when we take the time to get to know Jesus, when we hold Jesus' Body in our hands, when we spend time each week coming to His table to share in the meal Jesus has set out for us – we get to know Jesus a little bit better each time.

ART ACTIVITY: Hand out copies of Activity C

a. Explain this picture shows the table Jesus uses to put out his food for us. (Altar) Tell them every Catholic Church in the world has this table.

b. Have the students complete the sentence: I love you Jesus because_____:

c. Color and collect when completed.

Notes:

"So do not fear, for I am with you… I will uphold you with my righteous right hand."

(Isaiah 41:10)

DAY FOUR LESSON PLAN

GOAL: To integrate the book's message with the previous lessons

MATERIALS:

> A Handshake From Heaven book
> Copies of Activity D
> Pencils and Crayons/Markers
> Bag of 168 pieces of candy
> Previously completed art activities.

INTRODUCTION: Review previous lessons, using completed artwork to generate discussion if necessary.

a. Activity A: Remind students God knows all about us. He knew us before we were born. Ask them to remember some of the gifts God gave them. Ask them why adults shake hands.

b. Activity B: Ask them why we should come to His table. Why does God want to see us? Remind them of the bag of candy. Ask them why going to Mass is important to Catholics.

c. Activity C: Ask them what this picture means to them. What does the priest place on this table?

LESSON: Read and discuss A Handshake From Heaven,

ART ACTIVITY: Hand out copies of Activity D.

a. Using the book, show your students the page with Activity D's artwork.

b. Read the author's words for this Activity.

c. Have the students complete the sentence: **Jesus is my best friend because**:_____

d. Color and complete. Allow time for the students to finish any incomplete activity from previous lessons.

Notes:

"Be strong and courageous!... for the Lord your God is with you wherever you go."

(Joshua 1:9)

DAY FIVE LESSON PLAN

GOAL: To better understand the Eucharist as a gift Jesus gives us so we may know Him better..

MATERIALS:

A Handshake From Heaven book

Completed art activities

Copies of Activity E: *(Alternate activity, pass out blank paper and have the children write this sentence:* **This is what Heaven looks like to me**.)

Copies of Activity F: Book Cover Pages for students.

INTRODUCTION: Tell the students today they will put together their own Handshake book.

a. Reread A Handshake From Heaven to the class.

b. Remind them once again that the Eucharist is a gift Jesus gives to us because He wants us to get to know Him.

c. Remind them it does not matter what we look like, how we are dressed, if we are old or young. All Jesus wants is for us to come to his party, to His meal, and get to know Him.

d. Remind them Jesus wants us to know Him so we can be with Him in Heaven.

LESSON: Ask the students what they think Heaven looks like. Pass out Activity E. Have the students illustrate their vision of Heaven.

a. While students are completing this activity, collate and pass out their previous art activities, placing Activity F on top.

b. When students are finished, allow time to share their visions of Heaven.

c. Staple all art activities together. If time allows, have them color the cover of their book.

DISCUSSION: Have students return to group. Ask for volunteers to share their books.

a. Tell students we all have a choice to make: **Do we want to know Jesus?**

b. Then ask the students: "**If five birds are on a tree and one decides to fly away, how many are left?**"

> Most students will say four. Do it again with your one hand…"*If five birds are on a tree and one decides to fly away, how many are left?*" Again, many children will continue to say four.

> Continue by asking: "*One day you decide to surprise your mom and clean your room –Is it going to get clean just because you* decided *to clean it? Of course not! You have to decide to clean it and then actually clean your room! And just because a bird decides to fly away, doesn't mean he will actually leave the tree and fly away. Deciding to do something and doing it are two very different things.*

9

We can decide *to get to know Jesus, but in order to do that we have to actually come to His table!*

CONCLUSION: Demonstrate the sign language for the phrase: **Jesus I AM Here**.
- Middle finger of each hand to the opposite palm (Jesus)*
- Thumb to chest with the other fingers in a fist clench (I)*
- Thumb folded down onto palm, next three fingers over thumb, baby finger pointing away (M)*
- Hands outstretched, palms up. Keeping palms up, move hands in a circular motion once. (here) *
- End circular motion with one palm on top of the other.
- Place palms together, fingers pointing up. (Amen)*

reference: http://www.handspeak .com for video.

Have the student practice this with you a few times.

Then demonstrating alone, say:

1. "Jesus I AM Here because I want to get to know you better."
2. "Jesus I AM Here because I know you are the best friend I will ever have."
3. "Jesus I AM Here because I love you."
4. "Jesus I AM Here because I believe – Amen!"

Notes:

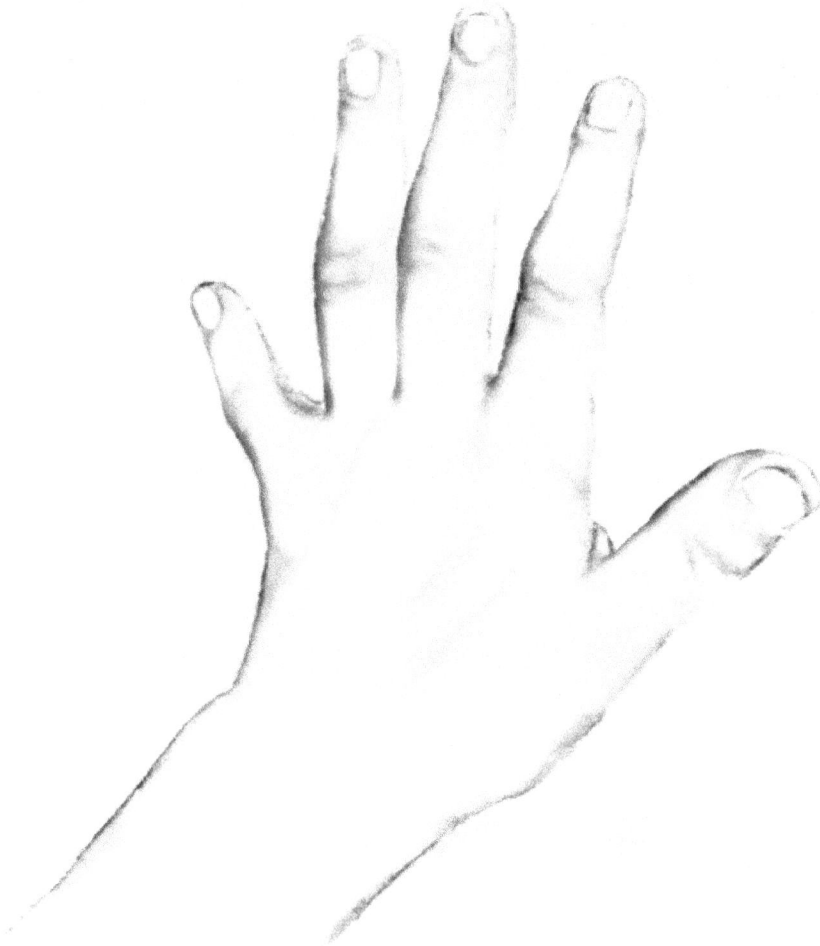

© handshake from heaven2006

I want to reach for Jesus because _____

_____

©handshake from heaven 2006

I will come to Your table because_____

_____.

Activity B

© handshake from heaven 2006

I love you Jesus because _____

_____.

Activity C

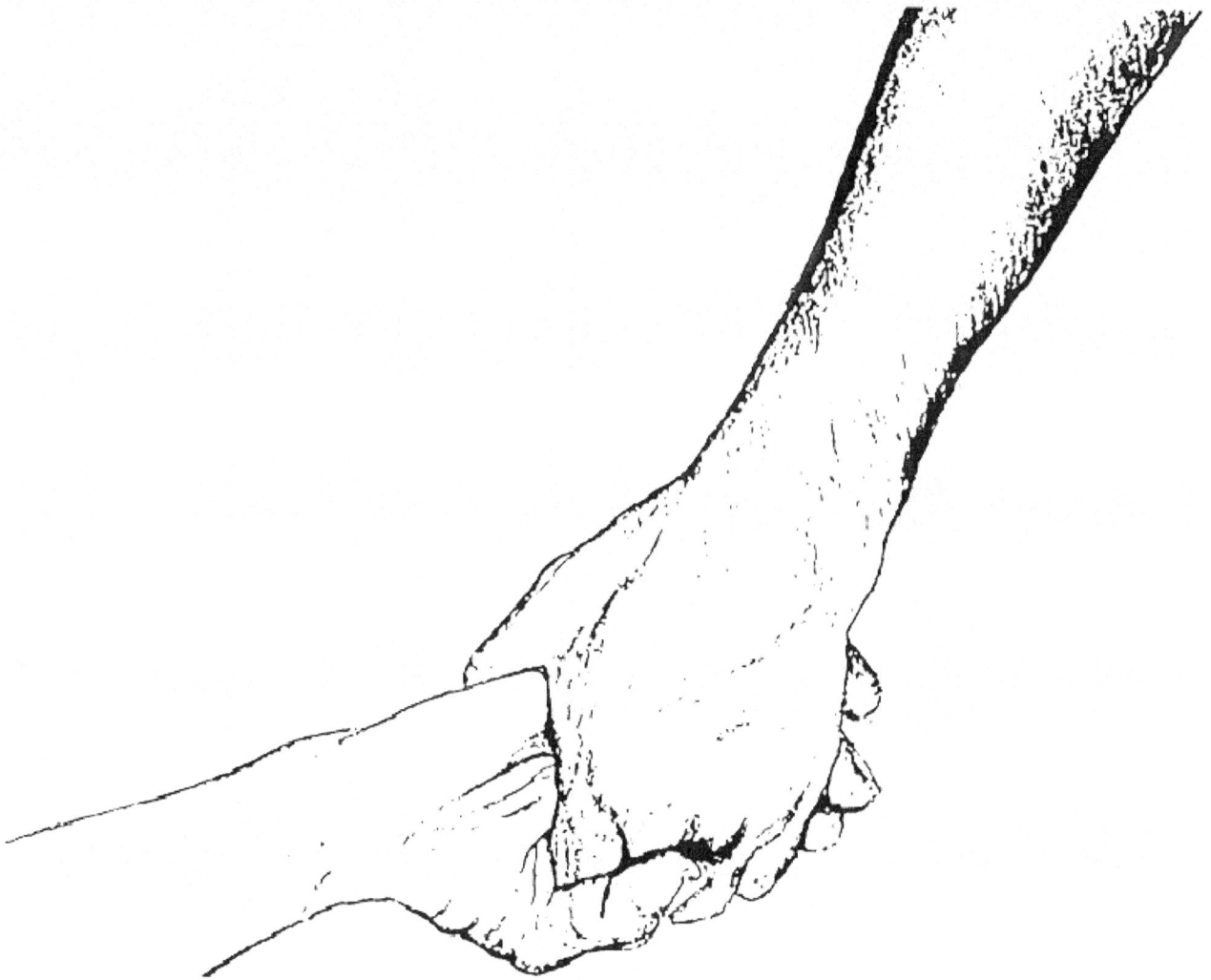

Jesus is my best friend because_____

_____.

Activity D

17

This is what Heaven looks like to me.

Activity E

Jesus and Me

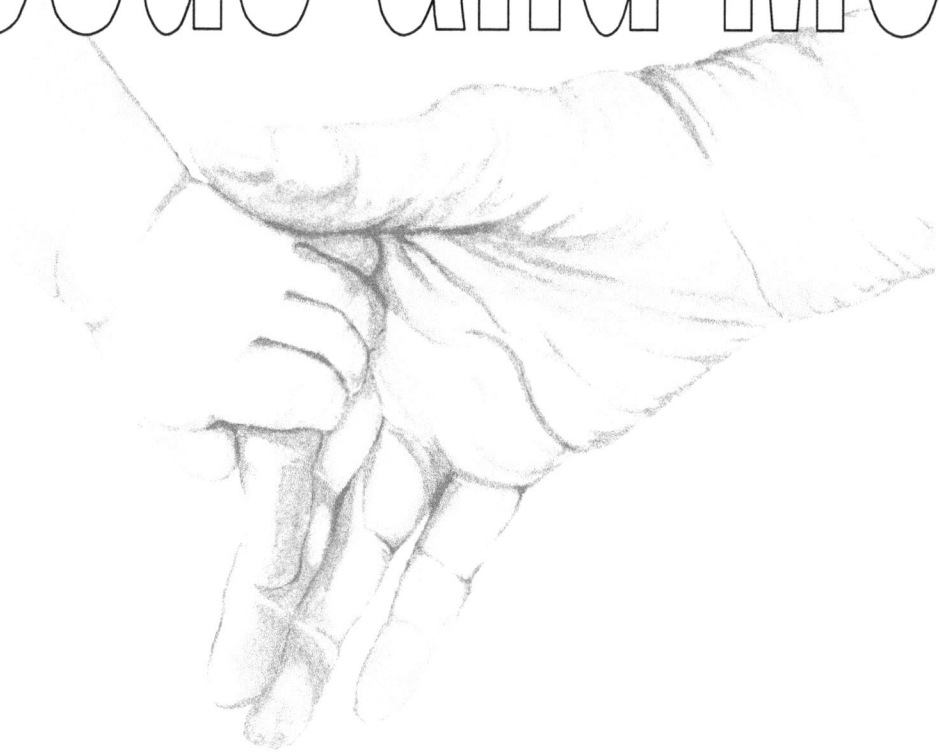

21

www.ingramcontent.com/pod-product-compliance
Lightning Source LLC
Chambersburg PA
CBHW081235020426
42331CB00012B/3185